His Love Letters
for Her

Robert H. Badgett III

Published by BookLocker.com, Inc., St. Petersburg, Florida, U.S.A.

Printed on acid-free paper.

BookLocker.com, Inc.
2017

First Edition

Introduction

To every mother, daughter, sister, aunt, cousin, friend-- to every woman who finds themselves flipping through the intimate pages of this book, it is my heart's desire that you discover real-truth. This truth can only be found in the one who is truth--God. As you take this journey with me, I ask that you find a quiet place to relax, sit back, and allow yourself to listen and embrace the words and affirmations that come from the Father, Son, Spirit and Husband.

These words and affirmations are an answer to the prayers I prayed, asking God for the wisdom and truth needed as I readily accepted my role as a father to my precious daughter. My heart's desire is to share God's truth and His wisdom with you.

As His daughter, you are precious in his sight-- beautifully and wonderfully made. I pray that you allow the message written throughout the pages of this book to put you in remembrance of that, as you open your heart to receive these personal love letters written with you in mind.

Dedication

In so many ways, my life changed when my little girl was born. Having witnessed women who have faced some of the most extreme challenges known to man, I found myself experiencing a myriad of emotions. Wanting what was best for her, and realizing just how tough life can be, I suddenly found myself feeling excited, anxious, proud and terrified, as I looked at my daughter for the first time.

Every father longs for his child to be successful in life- especially his daughter. He wants to protect her from all the wolves and evils of the world, while guiding and protecting her and her journey (as she searches for and discovers her identity and purpose)

Fathers play such a critical role in their daughter's life. It has been said that every little girl grows up and marries her daddy. This can feel like intense pressure to a dad who wants to set the best example for his daughter. In truth, I have not always been the best example. However, I have concluded that "greater is He that is in me, than he that is in the world." With God, all things are possible, and I can do anything if He gives me strength.

*As He provides me the courage, wisdom, and strength to be all that my daughter needs me to be, it's by His power and might that I leave the legacy of my words. They are words inspired by the one who has given me life and identity. He is the one who created us, and has the authority to identify our true-identity. He does this out of love-- for He is love. He truly loves us. How He chooses to express that love is a beautiful experience captured amongst the pages in this devotional. **His Love Letters for Her** is a thirty-one-day devotional message from the one who loves us unconditionally. Please allow me to share that love experience* *with you as I dedicate this book to my daughter Leniyah! "You will always choose well, when you make Him your choice".*

Love,
Daddy

The Father

Notes

My child, my daughter, my smile,
we have journeyed together for many miles.
There has never been a word that you spoke that
I did not hear.
I have always been present through the days of great
joy, and the nights of pillow stained tears.
My child, my daughter, my smile,
we have walked together for many miles.
I'm delighted to see me in your eyes.
You have searched for me, and I am your prize.

When life's challenges are great,
hide in me, for I am your escape.
My child, my daughter, my heart,
I have been with you from the start.
I'm satisfied with you, so from your heart, I
will never depart.
Replenish in me when you are weak; in my arms you
will find rest.
My child, my daughter, my smile,
out of all my creations, I have looked at you, and
concluded that you are my best.
-God

Day 1

My Daughter,

When I made heaven, I thought of you. I thought of how I would fashion you out of the rib of man. Before there was light, before there was day, before I spoke this world into existence, I had you in mind. I began by creating my son in my image, and from him you came. I watched as he watched over every living creature-naming them one by one; and yet something was still missing. It was you. For my will to be reproduced, I needed you to come into being. So, I put him to sleep, and began to form my good thing. I pulled you out of the rib of my son, so that he would always know that you are the balance within his being. Man, is not whole without woman. I shaped you in my glory. Your eyes are the window into the soul of the Earth. There are glimpses of heaven that peak out of you every time you blink. Your hands were created to be the gentle touch of love, and tenderness that keeps the peace in this world. I created you with insight and intuition. I loved making you. I smile when I look at your smile. You were made pure, and not touched by any human hand. When he awoke, there you were. He could see himself staring back at himself. He gazed in awe at your radiant splendor before him. How could he not love you? My presence was perfected in you. Patient, kind, sensitive, understanding, and compassionate. You were made beautiful. I made you.

-Your Heavenly Father

Do you know me?
Genesis 2: 22, Then the Lord God made a woman from the rib He had taken out of the man, and He brought her to the man.

_____

_____

_____

_____

_____

_____

_____

_____

_____

_____

_____

_____

_____

_____

_____

_____

_____

_____

_____

Day 2

My Little Girl,

I have watched you grow, and mature since you entered this world. It is my delight to see my light in you. You are so full of love. I am love, and I have made you like me. You are beautiful, dazzling and immaculate. I hold you in such high esteem. Your thoughts are my thoughts. Your ways are my ways. I enjoy the moments that we share in intimacy. I whisper the secrets and mysteries of my goodness into your ear, as we commune in our secret place. Life is in you. My child, my promises are always yes and amen. Dine with me daughter, and I will feed you my truth. Drink with me- my child- and I will fill you with my glory. In me you will always find you. Speak to me and I will hear you. Worship me and I will give more of myself to you. I will honor the dreams that I have placed inside of you. Seek me in the dark, and I will share my light.

-Your Heavenly Father

What are my plans for you?

Jeremiah 29: 11, "For I know the plans I have for you," declares the Lord, "plans to prosper you and not to harm you, plans to give you hope and a future".

_____

_____

_____

_____

_____

_____

_____

_____

_____

_____

_____

_____

_____

_____

_____

_____

_____

_____

Day 3

My Beloved Daughter,

    I welcome you into my presence. I have waited for you. You can trust me with your heart. I spoke you into existence; what task can I not fulfill? Give your dreams back to me, and I will produce good fruit. I treasure your thoughts, and I value your desires. Allow me to take you deeper. I'm acquainted with your intentions. There is no good thing that I will withhold from you, when you abide in me. I will always be your provider and comfort. Taste me and know that I am good. Test me and prove that I am faithful. I am your heavenly father. My love for you is endless.

-Your Heavenly Father

What does your heart desire?
Psalms 37:4, Take delight in the Lord, and He will give you the desires of your heart.

_____

_____

_____

_____

_____

_____

_____

_____

_____

_____

_____

_____

_____

_____

_____

_____

_____

_____

_____

_____

Day 4

Hello My Daughter,

I am here to love you. Show me your scars, and I will heal them. Hand me your heart, and I will protect it. I will secure you from your insecurities. Bring me your fears, and I will calm them. I know that you have been hurt, but my love will heal. I keep watch over you, even as you sleep. I will never leave you nor forsake you. I'm here to dry your tears. I am here to hug you when you hurt. I am the Lord --your Heavenly Father. Put your trust in me my child, and I will give you the desires of your heart. Make room for me, and I will come in. Lean into me, and I will give you rest. I am life. Let me breathe into you.

-Your Heavenly Father

How, and in what areas of your life, do you need me to love you?

Psalms 147: 3, He heals the brokenhearted, and binds up their wounds.

_____

_____

_____

_____

_____

_____

_____

_____

_____

_____

_____

_____

_____

_____

_____

_____

_____

_____

_____

Day 5

My Daughter --My Precious Child,

I am here. I'm proud of who you are. I have watched you grow, and become who I created you to be. Your beauty is striking; your words are my words. Let's go deeper, and I will show you more of me. Dance with me my daughter. You are fearfully and wonderfully made. Your hair, your eyes, your feet, and your nose -- all were made marvelously. I held you as a princess until you became a queen. I know that there have been moments when you have questioned your beauty. I feel your tears as they have dripped down your cheeks; but cry no more my sweet angel, your daddy is here. I am the calm in your storms; I am the shield against the winds. I am the "I am", and I am yours.

-Your Heavenly Daddy

Describe the beauty you see within yourself.
Psalms 139:14, I praise you because I am fearfully and wonderfully made; your works are wonderful, I know that full well.

Day 6

Hello My Daughter,

I call you destiny. My purpose and strength is made perfect in your weakness. I am your strength. Embrace me. Deposit my truth, and you will never be insufficient. Bask in my presence, and you will always be satisfied. Your skin was made from the clay and soil of the earth. You are mother of all the living. The sun sets on your back, and the moon rises at your feet. I know you, and understand your thoughts. I have searched you, and I am pleased with you. I will not hold your transgressions against you. You can run and hide in me. I will chase you in the green pastures. Death will not reign over you. I am aware of all your ways. I cherish the moments that we share together. I will not forget the details of the simple things. You are important to me.

Love,
Your Father

Where are you at in your life right now?

Jeremiah 29:12-13, 12 Then you will call on me and come and pray to me, and I will listen to you. 13 You will seek me and find me when you seek me with all your heart.

_____

_____

_____

_____

_____

_____

_____

_____

_____

_____

_____

_____

_____

_____

_____

_____

_____

_____

_____

Day 7

My Dearest Daughter,

You are my precious gift. I'm pleased with your desire to please me. There is no shame or guilt in me. I will not laugh at you, when you are vulnerable. I will not turn you away when you stumble. Here I am, you have searched and found me. You have asked, and I have answered. I am the Lord your God. Swim in my goodness, and become one with me. My sweet child, I will paint this world beautiful with you. I will use all that you are to saturate this world with my love. Share with me, and I will bear good fruit through you. Your children will call you blessed; the city will know of your great name. The groomsman will boast of your splendid ways. You are my daughter in whom I am well pleased.

-God

In what areas of your life have you tasted my goodness?

Psalms 34:4-8, 4 I sought the Lord, and he answered me;
he delivered me from all my fears.5 Those who look to him are radiant;
their faces are never covered with shame.6 This poor man called, and
the Lord heard him; he saved him out of all his troubles.7 The angel of
the Lord encamps around those who fear him, and he
delivers them.8 Taste and see that the Lord is good; blessed is the one who
takes refuge in him.

_____

_____

_____

_____

_____

_____

_____

_____

_____

_____

_____

_____

_____

_____

_____

_____

Day 8

My Dearest Daughter,

It will always be ok. In my arms, you will find rest. Put your trust in me my child. I understand exactly how you feel. There has never been a moment that I have not been with you, and there will never be a day that I will leave you. I love you.

-God

Has there ever been a time you have not felt secured in me?

Deuteronomy 31:6, Be strong and courageous. Do not be afraid or terrified because of them, for the Lord your God goes with you; he will never leave you nor forsake you.

_____

_____

_____

_____

_____

_____

_____

_____

_____

_____

_____

_____

_____

_____

_____

_____

_____

_____

_____

Notes

The Son

Notes

It was my
blood that dripped.
Back was whipped.
Clothes were stripped.
Skies did split.
On that day, I gave myself to you.
I would do it again and again.
For my sister, my friend,
my body did bend,
so, you would not be condemned.
Laying bare, limb to limb,
feet to brim,
weak to them,
strong in Him,
I love you!
What better price than a life?
Your wrongs covered in right?
A Father gave His son,
for a daughter who is such a beautiful one.
I am the way, the truth, and the life.
It was my privilege and pleasure to die and rise
So that you can have everlasting life.

-Jesus

Day 9

Hello My Sister,

I am the truth; there are no lies in me. Give me your hand, and I will walk with you. I have blotted out your transgressions, and replaced them with my love. Every scar, tear, and wound has been healed by my stripes. Don't let your heart be troubled my sister. I bled for you. I died and rose for you. You are valuable. As I laid on the cross, I endured it all for you. I have been, since the beginning. I engraved your name on my palms, to remind you that I will never let you go. In my Father's house, there is a room that has been made just for you. The bed has been prepared for you to rest. The mirror has been shaped to cast a pure reflection of your beauty. Bask in it. I'm overjoyed in knowing all that is waiting for you. It is our kingdom. To know me is to also know my Father; and our love for you is equal.

-Jesus

Do you know your worth to me?

John 14:6, Jesus answered, "I am the way and the truth and the life. No one comes to the Father except through me."

_____

_____

_____

_____

_____

_____

_____

_____

_____

_____

_____

_____

_____

_____

_____

_____

_____

_____

Day 10

My Beloved,

I have given you the power to do what I have done. I have kissed your hands with the same power that our Father has imparted into me. Use it for our glory. Lift me up, and I will draw all men unto me. Blessings will rain all over you, from your acts of service. You are clothed in humility, and I love it. Don't listen to the distractions that may come from the devourer. Remember my words, and all the great things that I have done for you, and for those before you. I will not fail you. Put your trust in me, and watch me fulfill my promise. You're His forever.

Love,
Your Savior

What have you been empowered to do?

John 12:25-26, 25 Anyone who loves their life will lose it, while anyone who hates their life in this world will keep it for eternal life. 26 Whoever serves me must follow me; and where I am, my servant also will be. My Father will honor the one who serves me.

_____

_____

_____

_____

_____

_____

_____

_____

_____

_____

_____

_____

_____

_____

_____

_____

_____

_____

Day 11

My Sister and Friend,

I heard you last night when you cried. I told you that I am with you. Remember my words when you are weak. Let me fight your battles. I am your strength. What more shall I show you, to let you know that my love is real? Consider my ways when you're in pain. Let us have communion, and you will be replenished. When your feet are tired, I will carry you. You were not designed to walk in this world alone. I will keep your secrets. You can tell me anything. Confess your transgressions, and I will forgive you. I know about the lies that you have been told, and I am the truth. I'm so proud of you. You're courageous and explosive. Be bold in all that you do. Don't ever forget who you are.

Love,
Jesus

Do you trust me? Why? Why not?

2 Corinthians 12:9, But he said to me, "My grace is sufficient for you, for my power is made perfect in weakness." Therefore, I will boast all the more gladly about my weaknesses, so that Christ's power may rest on me.

Day 12

Hello Queen,

How are you today? I've been thinking about you. Yes you. I have overcome the world to remind you that you can do the same. Today, is the day that you live again. New mercies have already been awarded to you. My grace is sufficient, and you are a priority. You were once blind, but now you have sight. You were lame, but now you're whole. I have healed you. There is nothing that you can't do. My word has been written in my blood. You have chosen me to walk with you, and you will receive a return on your investment. Whatever you ask in my name, will be given to you. I am the vine, and apart from me, you can do nothing. In me, you will bear good fruit. Our Father will cut off the dead branches and prune the good ones. You are well kept with us.

-Jesus

What can we do and accomplish together?

John 15:6-8, ⁶ If you do not remain in me, you are like a branch that is thrown away and withers; such branches are picked up, thrown into the fire and burned. ⁷ If you remain in me and my words remain in you, ask whatever you wish, and it will be done for you. ⁸ This is to my Father's glory, that you bear much fruit, showing yourselves to be my disciples.

_____

_____

_____

_____

_____

_____

_____

_____

_____

_____

_____

_____

_____

_____

_____

_____

Day 13

Our Father in Heaven,
Hallowed be your name.
Father, let your kingdom come,
And invade your daughters' world
Just as it is in heaven.
We only want your will to be done,
In every area that she walks on this Earth.
You have given her the day, and I am the bread.
Feed her.
Forgive all debts, and balance the scale with your goodness.
All debtors have been forgiven.
Keep her from temptation,
And deliver her daily from the evil one.
We thank you daddy!

-Your Son

What do you need from me?

Mathew 6:9-15, 9 "This, then, is how you should pray:
"'Our Father in heaven, hallowed be your name
, 10 your kingdom come, your will be done, on earth as it is in
heaven.11 Give us today our daily bread.12 And forgive us our debts, as
we also have forgiven our debtors.13 And lead us not into temptation, but
deliver us from the evil one.'14 For if you forgive other people when they
sin against you, your heavenly Father will also forgive you. 15 But if you
do not forgive others their sins, your Father will not forgive your sins.

_____

_____

_____

_____

_____

_____

_____

_____

_____

_____

_____

_____

_____

_____

_____

_____

Day 14

Dear Beautiful One,

I was born for you. My mother carried me nine months into this world, and knew that I was a gift. I'm the answer and the solution. I remember the day that they came for me. The word spread about my love for my Fathers children. They beat me. They spit on me, but I endured it for you. I felt every lash whipped into my flesh. For every blow that penetrated on my face, and every tear that trickled down my cheeks, it was all worth it. I would do it all over again. Some may wonder why our Father would allow such an act to occur to his only begotten son; but what is true love without a sacrifice? As I hung nailed to the cross, and bled onto the ground, I thought of your face. I thought of you gaining access to the kingdom. Your sins needed to be forgiven, and a sacrifice was in order. I was pierced for your transgressions. I was crushed for your iniquities. The punishment that brought you peace was on me, and my wounds healed you.

-Jesus

In what areas of your life do you feel bound and need me to set you free?

Isaiah 53:3-5, [3] He is despised and rejected of men; a man of sorrows, and acquainted with grief: and we hid as it were our faces from him; he was despised, and we esteemed him not.[4] Surely, he hath borne our griefs, and carried our sorrows: yet we did esteem him stricken, smitten of God, and afflicted.[5] But he was wounded for our transgressions, he was bruised for our iniquities: the chastisement of our peace was upon him; and with his stripes we are healed.

_____

_____

_____

_____

_____

_____

_____

_____

_____

_____

_____

_____

_____

_____

_____

_____

_____

_____

_____

Day 15

My Precious Jewel,

I will be with you until the ends of the earth. When you lay your head down at night, I will be with you. When you rise in the day, I will be with you. Take all that I have spoken, and eat it daily. Drink all of me, and leave nothing behind. Your cup is full. I'm the vine that has produced pure wine. I'm with you sister. I'm your friend; confide in me. Smile, your day has come. All authority in heaven and on earth has been given to me. It is your time to go forth and produce a body of disciples. You will baptize them in the name of my Father, and the Spirit that will arrive when I leave. I will be with you. Look inside when you cannot find me. I live in your heart. I love you, my sister, my friend.

-Jesus

What have you been called to do?

Mathew 28:18-20, [18] And Jesus came and spake unto them, saying, "All power is given unto me in heaven and in earth.[19] Go ye therefore, and teach all nations, baptizing them in the name of the Father, and of the Son, and of the Holy Ghost: [20] Teaching them to observe all things whatsoever I have commanded you: and, lo, I am with you always, even unto the end of the world." Amen.

_____

_____

_____

_____

_____

_____

_____

_____

_____

_____

_____

_____

_____

_____

_____

_____

_____

_____

Day 16

Beloved,

I am the vine and my Father is the gardener. Plant your desires in me, and you will bear great fruit. He will cut away the weeds and dead branches that choke away your richness. Your fruit will be fulfilling to all who eat it. They will taste and see that I am good. The rain will wash away all your imperfections. Delight in me and you will never spoil or wither away.

-Jesus

How Can I dress your heart, mind, body, and spirit today?

John 15:5, I am the vine, ye are the branches: He that abideth in me, and I in him, the same bringeth forth much fruit: for without me ye can do nothing.

_____

_____

_____

_____

_____

_____

_____

_____

_____

_____

_____

_____

_____

_____

_____

_____

_____

_____

Notes

Holy Spirit

Notes

Close your eyes, here I am.
I am the "I Am" in you.
Passion filled, power packed, wrapped in three, equally
reigning as one.
Resting in your bosom.
Father, Son, and
spirit, whispering sweetly, giving instruction.
Your guiding light in a world of corruption,
steal away with me, and be filled with no interruption.
Beloved, take more, and be restored.
My presence is perfect, and I decided that
you're worth it.
I want to live in you.
Worship, when the devourer wars against you.
Praise, when the pleasures of this world want to
persuade you away.
In the beginning, we were,
and in the end, we will be.
From heaven to earth, together forever,
We will spend in eternity.

-The Spirit

Day 17

My Dearest,

I reside in you. Listen to me, and I will lead you. Let me be your guiding light. Trust in my voice, and you will not be lead astray. I am the power that gives you power. Can you hear me? Can you feel me? I am your protection. Lean into me, and I will be your strength. Close your eyes and leap. There is nothing to fear. I am the whisper when the sounds are loud. Peace I bring to you.

-The Holy Spirit

What is blocking us from getting closer?

1 John 2:27, As for you, the anointing you received from him remains in you, and you do not need anyone to teach you. But as his anointing teaches you about all things and as that anointing is real, not counterfeit — just as it has taught you, remain in him.

Day 18

Hello,

I've been waiting for you. Come away with me. I am your secret place. Hide in me, and I will share my revelation with you. You have carried the weight long enough. I am the answer to all your questions. Lay down every stress and anxiety, and allow rest to take you over. Weep in this moment. We are in the deep together. I hear your heart aching, and I can feel your confusion. Be still, receive, and you will be filled.

-The Spirit

Tell me the things that matter to your heart.
2 Corinthians 3:17, Now the Lord is the Spirit, and
where the Spirit of the Lord is, there is freedom.

Day 19

Greetings My Dearest,

How are you? I have been waiting for you. This moment is about you. I was with you today, as I am every day. Don't forget what we spoke about. The answer is still yes. You have been walking in the will of the Father, and all your steps have been ordered. The outcome has been ordained and you have already won. You don't have to work anymore. I promise you this, there will be moments when my voice will become hard to hear. There may be even moments when trusting in what you cannot see is virtually impossible. But, if you stretch just a little, you will surely be rewarded. I know that it has been hard, and I know that you have wanted to quit, but you are victorious.

-The Spirit

What are some things keeping you from resting in me?

*Romans 8:26, In the same way, the Spirit helps us in
our weakness. We do not know what we ought to pray for, but the
Spirit himself intercedes for us through wordless groans.*

Day 20

To the Gifted Child,

Listen to me daughter. There is nothing wrong with you. Your features are stunning, and your smile is radiant. I want you to know that you are ok. I see the doubt, the fear, and I pull it out. The mind that was in Christ Jesus is also in you; which means that you are brilliant. You are not stupid or ugly. You are pretty, and amazing. We are so proud of you. They said that you were weird; we say that you are unique. They said that you are out of sync; we say that you are rightly related. The things that they have said about you are not from us. Don't believe in the lies that have come from the evil one. All your quirks are a part of who you have been created to be. Enjoy the gem that you are. I love you

Love,
The Spirit

How do you feel about yourself?

Psalms 139 :16, Your eyes saw my unformed body;
all the days ordained for me were written in your book before one of them
came to be.

Day 21

To My Sweet Dreamer,

The dream that you had last night was not a series of random thoughts and pictures. It was I who was speaking to you. I have been trying to get a message to you. Go deeper in me, and I will explain it to you. Pay attention to the sounds you hear, and the pictures that I am showing you. Nothing is by coincidence. Chance does not exist when you are walking in purpose. You have not missed it. I need you to focus. This is very important, and I need you to hear me. I desire real intimacy with you. But, for us to have communion, I need you to blot out the distractions. Now, is not the time to starve me and feed your flesh. Now is the time to starve your flesh and feed me. Put your mind to sleep and awaken your heart. Here I am. shhhhhh.

-Holy Spirit

What are you dreams?
Psalms 139:7, Where can I go from your Spirit? Where can I flee from your presence?

_____

_____

_____

_____

_____

_____

_____

_____

_____

_____

_____

_____

_____

_____

_____

_____

_____

_____

_____

_____

Day 22

Fear not my dear!

I know you're afraid. But you don't have to be. Your fear has kept you from relying on my power. You will gain nothing in your own strength. I want you to trust me. I'm not offended by your weakness. It is in your weakness that my strength makes you sufficient. You will fail without me. You will always succeed with me. Don't waste any more time trying to do it your way. I'm here --trust in me. I have you.

-Holy Spirit

Tell me all your fears!

Jeremiah 29:11, For I know the plans I have for you," declares the Lord, "plans to prosper you and not to harm you, plans to give you hope and a future.

_____

_____

_____

_____

_____

_____

_____

_____

_____

_____

_____

_____

_____

_____

_____

_____

_____

_____

_____

Day 23

Dear Sweet Child,

My arms are open. I'm here to receive you. My love is real, and it is perfect. It cast out all fear. Embrace me, and be restored. I know that you have sinned, but you have been forgiven. I hear the truth and conviction that is in your heart. Your words have confessed, and your transgressions have been forgiven. You don't have to live in shame or guilt any longer. Raise your head daughter, and fix your gaze. You have been established and you can now begin again.

-The Spirit

Tell me the things you need forgiveness for.
*1 John 1:9, If we confess our sins, He is faithful and just
and will forgive us our sins and purify us from all unrighteousness.*

Notes

Your Husband

Notes

I'm gasping for your air, breathe into me.
Your Love-clouds shower down raindrops of ecstasy.
Become my wind.
Inhale, exhale, I want more;
Again, I say Again!
My sweet sleep arrives when we collide.
I'm a Lion tamed by your affection.
Stroke me with your goodness.
Your eyes calm the raging waves crashing
within my soul.
I'm whole with you.
I rest with you until daybreak.
We awake in the peaceful silence of today.
Our hearts playfully give chase as we escape
into green pastures.
Laughter fills the air.
Cuddling in the comfort of tranquility.
Intimate isolation fills the atmosphere.
Fear departs as faith empowers.
Here we are, you
and I Forever!
-Your Lover

Day 24

Hello My Blessing,

I adore you for all that you are. Our Father created me to love you. It is my desire to do nothing less. My soul has become one with you. I studied you, and I am acquainted with your ways. Smile, and I will take notice; laugh and I will be filled with delight. You are all that I have prayed for-- my beloved. Let us escape into forever after. Lay your head on my heartbeat. Tell me your secrets, and I will guard them with my life. I will protect your heart. Bury your treasures in me.

-Your Lover

What more can I give to you?
*1 Corinthians 11:11-12, 11 Nevertheless, in the Lord woman
is not independent of man, nor is man independent of woman.
12 For as woman came from man, so also man is born of woman.
But everything comes from God.*

Day 25

My Desire,

I'm running after you. I'm gasping for air. Breathe into me with your affection. I want to find rest in your heart. I can see His love in your eyes. Your beauty captivates me. You are my queen, and I am your king. Let us rule together. We have been given dominion, and we shall reign as one. My beautiful bride, I am amazed by you. You have stolen my heart, and I shall not ask you to return it. I am yours forever.

-Your Husband

What do you want for our future?

Proverbs 18:22, He who finds a wife finds what is good and receives favor from the Lord.

_____

_____

_____

_____

_____

_____

_____

_____

_____

_____

_____

_____

_____

_____

_____

_____

_____

_____

_____

_____

Day 26

My Darling,

   I have dreamed about you all day. I have fantasied about your kiss. Your caramel, honey scent, soothes the tip of my nose. Your eyes casts a glimpse of His glory. You walk with confidence, and security. I feel your passion. I want to run my fingers through your hair, and caress your thoughts. Rest your breast upon me, and let the day waste away. Give me your undivided attention, and I will bare my soul. Here I am my love. I want nothing else but you. You are more than enough. My arms are open my darling-- receive my sweet embrace. I will never let go.

-Him

Am I safe with you?

Songs 6:5, Turn your eyes from me; they overwhelm me. Your hair is like a flock of goats descending from Gilead

_____

_____

_____

_____

_____

_____

_____

_____

_____

_____

_____

_____

_____

_____

_____

_____

_____

_____

_____

Day 27

My Beloved Air,

My sweet heartbeat, I can feel your pain, I see your scars, and I still want you. Dry your tears on my collar, and weep on my chest. This is your moment, and I will not reject you. I can hear your silent screams. Empty out your heartache and let me fill you with joy. You don't have to hurt any longer. I 'm here. You have permission to display total vulnerability. I promise you sanctuary. I am a safe place. Come hide in me. You can trust me with your wounds. He sent me to love you. My love is unconditional. Bleed out and become cleansed. I LOVE YOU.

-Your Protector

Tell me your truth!
Genesis 1:27, So, God created mankind in his own image, in the image of God he created them; male and female he created them.

Day 28

My Love,

I will provide in every way possible. Cast your fears on the one who cares, and rely on me. Lover, you can confide in me, and I will listen. Speak to me. I will meet your needs, and support you with love and affection. Your steps are ordered; walk into your destiny. Your purpose has been written in the sands of time. I'm persuaded by your ambition. Your hunger for truth is infectious. Your appetite for righteousness is appealing. You are my queen, and I will cover you. I am your champion that will cheer you on. Run after your dreams. I am running with you.

-Your Provider

What do you need from your man?

Ephesians 5: 25-26, [25] Husbands, love your wives, just
as Christ loved the church and gave himself up for her[26] to make her holy,
cleansing her by the washing with water through the word.

_____

_____

_____

_____

_____

_____

_____

_____

_____

_____

_____

_____

_____

_____

_____

_____

Day 29

Queen,

Today I spent time interceding for you. I roared in worship for my beloved. I sought out the secret place, with you in my heart. Lay down, and I will wash you in His word, and cleanse you in prayer. As the Father leads me, I will lead you. The vision for our union is clear. He has breathed new life into us, and we are predestined for greatness. You are a virtuous gift sent from the giver.

-Your Priest

What are your prayers for us?
Songs 7: 6, How beautiful you are and how pleasing, my love,
with your delights!

_____

_____

_____

_____

_____

_____

_____

_____

_____

_____

_____

_____

_____

_____

_____

_____

_____

_____

Day 30

Heavenly Father,

Daddy God, I humbly submit my life before your thrown. I lift my beloved to you. Lord, I ask that you pour your love into me, so that I may love her appropriately. I lay my life down for your daughter. I present my body as a living sacrifice. Just as your son did, I also lay my life down for my bride. God, strengthen me with your words, so that I may speak loving truth. I speak vision into her life. I speak courage and passion. I declare that she will prosper in you. Guard her from the evil one. Make her a great nation. Let your will be done, on earth, as it is in heaven. You call her virtuous and blessed. Be the center of us, in all that we say and do. In Jesus name, Amen.

-Your Covering

What do you want to express to your beloved?

Genesis 2:20-24, [20] So the man gave names to all the livestock, the birds in the sky and all the wild animals. But for Adam no suitable helper was found. [21] So the Lord God caused the man to fall into a deep sleep; and while he was sleeping, he took one of the man's ribs and then closed up the place with flesh. [22] Then the Lord God made a woman from the rib he had taken out of the man, and he brought her to the man.[23] The man said, "This is now bone of my bones and flesh of my flesh; she shall be called 'woman,' for she was taken out of man."[24] That is why a man leaves his father and mother and is united to his wife, and they become one flesh.

_____

_____

_____

_____

_____

_____

_____

_____

_____

_____

_____

_____

_____

_____

_____

Day 31

Dance with me my darling,

Heaven has rewarded me with you. Let me lead the way. Rest your hands on my shoulders, and your head on my chest. I will whisk you away in sweet matrimony. The floor is ours, and we are alone. Dance with me my darling --until forever ends. Let your body move to the sweet melody of our heartbeat.

-Your Leader

Describe your happily ever after.

Song of Solomon 6: 8-9, ⁸ Sixty queens there may be, and eighty concubines,
and virgins beyond number;⁹ but my dove, my perfect one, is unique,
the only daughter of her mother, the favorite of the one who bore her.
The young women saw her and called her blessed; the queens
and concubines praised her.

_____

_____

_____

_____

_____

_____

_____

_____

_____

_____

_____

_____

_____

_____

_____

_____

Notes

Expressions to my daughter
Leniyah, Imani, Badgett

Notes

For my Daughter,

My sweet pudding, I remember the day like it was yesterday. Mommy and I had a dream about you on the same day, at the very same time. I saw you before you came out. I prayed that God would bless me with a little girl. I spoke you into existence. I saw your pretty, round, brown face. Your eyes were bold and beautiful. I'm the luckiest daddy in the world. You make me smile princess.

Love,
Daddy

My Pretty Girl,

You almost didn't make it out of mommy's tummy. Mommy was rushed to the hospital, and the doctors told us that mommy was not going to be able to keep you. We prayed, and I declared that you were going to come, and nothing in this world was going to stop that! I put my hand on mommy's belly and said, "In the name of Jesus, your wound is healed, and Leniyah will come into this world." Amen. Guess what happened next? You came! It was one of the best days of my life. You were such a good baby girl. I knew that you were just like me, and I was so proud to call you mine.

Love,
Papa

Leniyah, Imani, Badgett,

Your name means God is our light, and our faith. We knew that you came as a child of faith. Don't ever forget who you are, and what your name means. You are royalty, and your steps have been ordered. I pray for you every day. I have faith that God will protect and guide you. In this life, people will call you many things, but that does not matter. What matters most is what you answer to. Don't ever forget who you are.

Love,
Daddy

My Special Girl,

You are gifted. God made you special. You remind me so much of myself. You are creative and very precocious. The way your mind works is fascinating to me. You are very aware, alert, and smart. Some people will never understand you. That's ok. But it's important that you share your genius with the world. Don't ever hold back your strengths. I want you to shine bright in a dark world. Your pretty smile lights up the room when you enter. I'm so proud of everything that you are.

Love,
Your Father

Ms. Leniyah,

Today, you became a woman. I'm truly terrified -- to say the least. You will always be my child, but you are no longer a baby. You have been predestined for greatness. This world is big, but our God has given you dominion. It is yours to rule, as He reigns. Hold onto the teachings that have been imparted to you over the years. I believe in you baby. Go for it!

Love,
Dad

Notes

CPSIA information can be obtained
at www.ICGtesting.com
Printed in the USA
LVHW02s2247251018
594796LV00001B/187/P